THE BUTTERFLY GARDEN AND
12 OTHER POEMS OF THE YEAR

THE BUTTERFLY GARDEN
AND 12 OTHER
POEMS OF THE YEAR

BY

WAYNE K. CHAPMAN

CLEMSON
UNIVERSITY
PRESS

Clemson University Press, 2025

ISBN 978-1-63804-224-2

CLEMSON
UNIVERSITY
PRESS

Typeset in Adobe Garamond Pro
by the poet & Charis Chapman

Acknowledgments

The South Carolina Review 57.1 (Fall 2024) for "The Butterfly Garden";
The Virginia Woolf Miscellany 102 (Fall 2024) for "The Woolfs on the
Notion of Zot" and "The Woolfs on Tides"

Esteemed readers: Diane Gillespie, Martin Jacobi, Neil Mann, Keith Morris, Vara
Neverow, Catherine Paul, Pat Rawlinson, and Bob Spoo

Cover design and photography by Charis Chapman. Apple illustration
from a historic advertisement, "See Graton and Green Valley, Center
of the Famous Gravenstein Apple Section"; the poet makes applesauce
each year from the abundant harvest of an heirloom grafting of
Gravensteins. Illustration of a Bourgeau rose is plate 344 in Mary Vaux
Walcott, *North American Wild Flowers*, vol. 5 (1925). Butterfly-net
doodle from Samuel Hubbard Scudder, *Brief Guide to the Commoner
Butterflies of the Northern United States and Canada* (1893).

CONTENTS

This book is for Marilyn, Charis, and Will.

The Butterfly Garden

It is fourteen February
twenty twenty-four,
feast of Saint Valentine,
Leap Year, and Year of
Chinese dragons, stuff
and simple nonsense.

On a low heather bush,
beneath our front window,
a hummingbird tries its
courage while a neighbor
cat (biding its time and
craving this bird) waits.

The hummingbird hovers
and darts over that clump
of heather, with snow drops
and crocuses blooming in
the yard to help rekindle
the old butterfly garden.

The butterfly bush is dead,
and heather leavens the sight
of cold mud in the rain
(ashes to ashes as it were),
mauve blotches arrayed
like promises on wiry stems.

The cat waits, cannot know
the breeding imperatives
of a hummingbird in winter
because it makes no sense,
winding the springs of one's
haunches to leap at a crumb.

Cat jumps; the bird escapes—
Amen.

Getting Doored at 73

That is to say we got totally "doored" while parked, curb-side, in our no-frills Nissan Versa—meaning we were lucky, as defined by the infinitive *to door*, a cyclist's transitive verb for a door that opens and bashes one in an act of collision (present participle, *dooring*; simple past and past participle, *doored*; and third-person singular simple present, *doors*).

Since I was in the driver's seat, it was my arm that might have been lost, but wasn't, to the white Lexus with expired plates. The door buckled and swooshed out, suddenly gone, leaving our car open like a helicopter cockpit without a door, the Lexus sliding by at a runner's clip, 12-15 miles per hour, I would guess, and stopping at the end of a tinny screech,

not the sound that a real car might have made 50 years ago, as I remember, but a thin sound. Stop-motion, expletive mine. Dooring and doored, as agent and victim, are a bad business for automobiles no less than for people, in this case related inversely to the custom of speech applied to a man or woman on a bicycle vis-à-vis two people, parked, one opening a door.

A car is not a bicycle (I shall not grieve) but a day forfeited is still a day's happiness lost to the opening of a door, to trading information between moving and nonmoving drivers, and to the ordeal by cell phone to get the car home by tow and then to hospital, the broken door tied back to a window-post as in a sling (poor car). Injury is hard to assess when both cars are hurt.

So this is my ode to getting doored at 73, after 58 years on the roadway (small comfort), when parking on a congested street. Of course *to open* is another transitive puzzle when it takes a reflexive in conjunction with the noun *door*, for example, in the sentence "The door opened itself," or "The door did not open because car doors cannot open themselves." Semantics.

The Last House

A house deserves a name when it becomes
the last house you expect to own or occupy.
La dernière maison sounds dull, too *passé*
simple. But then French is a literature, not
a language that I have studied cheerfully, as
I have the English of numerous Irish writers.
An teach deireanach means the final house.
But how to avoid discord in mitigating fault,
a slur to the merit of an old mother tongue?

On Turning 74

With Swift, there's probably not much
to rave about if the brain is not actually
famished but sentient and enough alive
still to do one's work reasonably well,
not every day, perhaps, but most and for
as long as one can manage in principle.

A birthday lyric is at least a work in
progress, a whole defined by simple x
and y, a life split into seven spans of
a bridge sustained by rib arches five
(student, father, teacher, editor, writer),
to liken y in 5xy to the coefficient 5x.

Make no mistake, sometimes lessons
have to be difficult. As a child, I often
wondered if school would ever end (it
doesn't), and later on, except for sports,
I was a perplexed learner working in
fields and under cars, behind a library

circ desk on work-study, or processing
i.d. cards and liquor licenses for the state
while tasked to form a bridgehead from
experience—a marriage, an intermezzo
of trekking across seven European states
in as many months, touring monuments,

lidos, open country, and posting home
diapositives to account—then saving up
by doing more such clerking by day and
academic studies by night, counting on
77.5 years of expected life but not a wit
less than the median 74 years of certain

paternal ancestors. Undependably, time
lurks around that threshold, indefinitely
offering perhaps the other 3.5 years for
whatever thing I might still have in me
to do. When fatherhood happened twice,
at 32 and 37, accentuating serious study,

an era began with a daughter and son
to herald the story's technical climax,
as if life happens in discrete phases to
a scholarly novice determined to teach
brash freshmen and worried to support
a family in a superannuated profession.

A son myself, I find the role enduring.
On losing parents, one keeps on being
that son. My daughter and son are lucky,
I think, because I remember the child I
was and still am because of them. In all
candor, it puts a fine point on learning.

But for some reason, the architecture
held: the bridge rose mostly as planned
with the rest history, a matter of books
edited and submitted; books, essays, and
chapters written, published, and laid out
abstractly in an updated curriculum vita.

Thus another 37 years came and went.
My father died at 74, as did his mother,
as well as did the Irish poet W. B. Yeats,
on whose life and work my career built
an enterprise without adding much profit.
In the end, what truly matters is how one

is remembered, if at all, by peers whose
values one shares and who find in one's
work something to perpetuate their own
in the common interest of a great topic.
For living a good life so far, I should say
happy birthday to me—with more anon.

That said, I will add a *coda* for my wife
and partner of fifty years, in many ways
my muse, likeness of *Olympia* in the Jeu
de Paume. Hard of hearing, I was taught
never to shirk a debt. Yet my eyes behold
in hers the value of wisdom unreproved.

The Woolfs on the Notion of Zot

At 5:40 a.m. PDT, twenty May twenty
twenty-four; hardly a minute before
sunrise at Spanish Head, Siletz Bay,
Oregon (44° 57' 32" N / 124° 0' 48" W);
I see the sky and ocean engulfed, or
englobed as we say in Woolf studies,
failing to recall that *two* Woolfs merit
credit for much the same perception.

Let us call it "Zot" as the last increment
before zero in the countdown from night,
the last to reveal its place before daylight
invades the latter with a hooplike glow
relative to all four points of the compass
or wheel of life. A poet friend of Virginia
Woolf and Joyce and Pound once wrote
that they seemed of the Samkara school

of India, such that they wrote as if to melt
"limits of line or tint [like] a swimmer, or
rather the waves themselves." The implied
comparison between *Fighting the Waves*
(1932) and Woolf's *The Waves* (1931) left
Yeats a bit short of her mark as a modernist,
perhaps, although she took the compliment
well. *The Waves* begins by painting in italics:

"*The sun had not yet risen. The sea was
indistinguishable from the sky, except that
the sea was slightly creased as if a cloth had
wrinkles in it.*" As the sky whitened, the sun
rose and fell like a lamp with the progress
of characters, by turns, making the novel
until she completes the circle of their lives,
jousting Death, waves breaking on a shore.

A found agate milled in the surf with a piece
of shell shaped like a shark's tooth, very like
the ones pitched by waves on sandy beaches
in the Carolinas, is here a pebble quarried as

such from a vein in lava rock and pounded
for aeons. Across the vast Pacific, in a pearl
fishery in Ceylon, Leonard Woolf observed
the death of a diver before the light of day—

how the Arab's fellows were "motionless,
somber, mysterious, part of the grey sea,
of the grey sky" until "dawn broke red in
the sky." Leonard wrote in this Conradian
narrative, "Pearls and Swine," that "over
the shoulders of the men I saw the feet
of the dead man with the toes sticking up
straight and stark." Dawn grew from that.

Forty years on, he cribbed the story in his
Autobiography to show how the "bearded
face of the dead man looked very calm,
very dignified in the faint light," omitting
the Tamil proverb: "When the cat puts his
head into a pot, he thinks all is darkness."
Yet the volume began with a hopeful scene:
a second birth by sailing from Tilbury Docks

down the Thames for Ceylon, severing the
umbilical cord attached to family, St. Paul's,
and Cambridge in a "dirty, dripping murk"
of river fog to the Channel, where "it was
barely possible to distinguish the cold and
gloomy sky from the cold and gloomy sea."
In retrospect, the lived moment, this Zot,
viewed from the taffrail of the P & O *Syria,*

portended, as twilights tend to do, "strange
experience" that would leave "a permanent
mark" on his character in starting out anew
for a place both "menacing and depressing."
Such moments are the percepts of magical
thinking, Bloomsbury humanism, Irish poets,
and creative mystics wherever we find them.
Yet what creatures we all are, at last. *O Life!*

The Woolfs on Tides

In 1914, Leonard and Virginia Woolf lived in
Richmond upon Thames, and in six months
moved to Hogarth House on Paradise Road.
Coincidentally, on the other side of the planet,
my grandmother's family began leasing a dairy
on the North Fork of the Siuslaw River when
there was no road to town (Florence, Oregon)
and the river was the highway to civilization.

My mother's mother's mother rowed to teach
Sunday school at Portage, near Morris Creek.
The tribe named after the river (and vice versa)
had been relocated up the coast beyond Heceta
Head and the brood caves of sea lions that they
hunted for food to supplement a diet of salmon
and edible wild plants. Seal oil lubricated the
machinery of numerous steam-driven sawmills.

The Woolfs too understood the tides from plain
sight, the ebb and flow viewed on a riverwalk
at Kew Gardens or from the deck of a ferryboat
to Westminster Pier, though not from seafaring
and shipbuilding in the Docklands as have some
who left but then turned up on the Pacific coast
of the US, dodging logs that drift both ways on
the North Fork with seasonal shifts at the mills.

Roughly every twelve hours (but often more or
commensurably less) the sea crests or troughs
on a coastline from the pull of the Moon's orbit
around the Earth in a cycle of highs and lows
only somewhat delayed by dangerous currents
and sandbars at the mouths of winding channels.
Leonard Woolf will have had his charts and tide
tables with him during Customs duty in Jaffna.

There a man died by going too long on a breath,
working the shoals of lagoons for oyster pearls
at a Shakespearean depth of five fathoms when
the winds were unfavorable. As all the waves of

the sea belonged to England, *ergo:* all breeding oysters at the bottom of the sea (and especially their pearls) "belong to us," Leonard's persona avers facetiously to his foils in one short story.

In the Jaffna, Kandy, and Hambantota chapters of *Growing (1904-1911)*, Woolf rarely refers to lunar tides except by inference or allusion. For example, "because the town and peninsula are almost completely shut in on [Jaffna's] west by islands," he remembers best "a pink line of flamingos wading in the shallow waters" rather than tidal effects, other than an *ennui* conveyed

to him by waves lifting themselves up at regular intervals, "slowly, wearily" lifting in silence, until falling monotonously with a "great thud," as if mimicking official duties. Even beautiful Celestinahami, in "A Tale Told by Moonlight," is left to drown and be found intact, "floating in the sea that lapped the foot of the convent garden below the little bungalow—bobbing up

and down in her stays and pink skirt and white stockings and shoes." Like a full Moon she is a literary trope, an exotic fixture of romance, yet one that seems almost fateful in retrospect. As a minimalist by comparison, Virginia Woolf is in fact more observant on tidal confluences. In *The Waves,* for instance, the sea is "*barred with thick strokes moving, one after another,*

beneath the surface," following and pursuing "*each other, perpetually,*" the bars becoming log-like (suggesting sound, perhaps) as colors in the sky's palette begin to infuse one's eye with a light that absorbs trees in the garden. In the course of a day (the collective lifetimes of characters who are at first children), objects emerge and submerge, and the sea surges into

"*a cave that had been dry before*" and leaves pools "*where some fish, stranded, lashed its tail as the wave drew back.*" As the sun sinks,

we still have the white shadows of waves in
"*the recesses of sonorous caves*" rolling "*back
sighing over the shingle.*" With darkness, the
novel ends on a grace-note offered in simple
past tense: "*The waves broke on the shore.*"

Six persons become an absence of presence in
this tableau while the sea remains animate but
subject to the weather and the laws of Newton,
wherein every twelve hours (give or take) the
sea must crest or trough, by turns, as Earth, di-
urnally, and Moon, nocturnally, dance in empty
space in synchronic relation to the Sun, driving
the winds and, as we have here, a still-busy surf.

It is also apt that *To the Lighthouse*, Virginia's
roman à clef based on Stephen family holidays
in Cornwall (not the Hebrides), should ring true
nautically in various respects. First, she shows
that crossing the bar in an open boat depends on
more than fair weather in dramatizing by delay
the Ramsay expedition to a singular lightstation
off the Isle of Skye (but actually the Godrevy

Lighthouse of St. Ives Bay—although it might as
easily have been the Heceta Coast Guard station)
to make her point about a mariner's concern for
submerged obstacles. There is a sunken vessel
to see as one passes over—an unreality to reckon
with the tide as the sea becomes "more important
now than the shore," to Cam (to Virginia as she
remembers herself), with "a log wallowing down

one wave" and a seagull riding another one on
the exact spot where "a ship had sunk" and she
(Cam) echoes her father, "dreamily, half asleep,
how we perish, each alone." And, finally, how
well Virginia writes about Macalister's piloting
the boat with young James Ramsay (*i.e.* Adrian
Stephen) steering it, "like a born sailor," to the
lighthouse, her late-father "leaping into space"

on the rock!

The Marabar Caves and Such Fantasies

In my view, caves are best left to themselves.
Native peoples near the Rogue and Applegate
Rivers for 8,500 years, down to the nineteenth-
century Takelma tribe, evidently made no use
of the marble caves of the Siskiyou Mountains;
and though I entered those cold passages *once*,
in 1957, I could not bring myself to do it again,
as a fully grown man, twenty-three years later.

The year before I shunned the gateway to Belly
of the Whale and the labyrinthine passage to
Miller's Chapel and the Ghost Room, I swam
200 yards across a lagoon on Corfu and into
one of Pan's seacaves as Douglas Fairbanks's
brazen Pirate might have done for an imagined
treasure buried in sand 33 cubits into the vault,
slightly higher in the throat than at its mouth.

The skull can be a cave when scale is relative.
Nausica's cave at Paleokastritsa took all my
heart as my wife waved from across the *plage*.
Still, for a child of seven, the OCNM (Oregon
Caves National Monument) weighed heavily—
the force of tons radiating as so many invisible
g's out of colossal stone, a mountain bearing
down, metamorphosed from a calcitic seabed

that arose with tectonic movement below but
also weighed down on one in unfinished form
as a "solutional cave" with passages dissolved
by water and strewn with fossils of grizzly bear,
mountain beaver, jaguar, and various species
of blind amphibians 4,000 feet above sea-level
and in absolute darkness. On finding the caves
in 1874, exploration began in candlelight ("*ma*

lampe qui sait pourtant mon agonie," a French
poet said). When the guide shut off the lights
for 60 seconds in Watson's Grotto, I counted
silently to remain calm. Similarly, in Forster's
A Passage to India, darkness and acoustics are
agitative agents to be countenanced, reflexively,
by the lighting of a match. Yet slight sound is
amplified in the Marabar Caves with a deadly

effect upon the Western mind, reverberating
within the eardrum beyond the accustomed
scratch of a match or click of an English torch
to start "a little worm coiling" in the cochlea
to become "'Boum' [...] as far as the human
alphabet can express it, or 'bou-oum,' or 'ou-
boum'"—a symptom of auditory transduction
without benign paroxysmal positional vertigo.

Unlike the organ-like pipes of the OCNM's
vertical stalagmites and stalactites, the means
of echoing in the Marabar Caves is attributed
to their spherical form and exceptional polish,
indicative of the "Nothing" that is attached to
them, the Nothing inside them, the gods and
ghosts of the Marabar Hills. The caves are as
empty as an Easter egg, somebody's *le néant.*

The crux belongs to two women, an old Mrs.
Moore and an adventure-seeking Miss Adela
Quested, whose crises engender two of the
novel's parallel plots and impart additional
mysteries upon the caves. "Esmiss Esmoor"
stands for the Empire's belief in England's
duty to be pleasant to her subject people, but
"a terrifying echo" displaces that faith with

a view in which everthing exists and nothing
has value. Similarly, when Quested drops her
field glasses, the novel's climax comes about
because she panics, feels "bottled-up," when
nothing but an echo actually happens to her.
The dramatic action materializes from a trick
played by the author on his readers, which is
that the Marabar Caves don't actually exist.

"Visions are supposed to entail profundity, but— Wait till you get one, dear reader!" He visited the Barabar Hill Caves in 1913, the oldest, rock-cut structures in India and, even then, popular tourist attractions in the Jehanabad district—four caves dating from the Maurya Empire of 322-185 BCE—each one carved out of solid granite and polished

to such a luster as to produce an echo; two caves are inscribed with the names of kings and so are hardly prehistoric or monumental in the sense of the OCNM, though Forster imparted to them rare geologic features that one associates with pseudo-natural wonders. That is, his caves are circular chambers, like bubbles, apart from countless others "deeper

in the granite [that] have no entrances" and have never been "unsealed since the arrival of the gods"—bubbles with neither ceilings nor floors that somehow mirror their "own darkness in every direction infinitely," as ancient mythology posits the creation of first forms from Chaos and the Void, Eros and Anteros out of the wind-egg of Night.

In the end, we have a psychologically true but occult fable about people who try but fail to understand one another in a country riddled with social and political fissures, very like the build-up to a seismic event but not like the low subterranean throb of marble seams along Oregon's Cave Creek as it drips into the head as the River Styx.

The Marabar, like the novel and its Hindu sources in the Barabar and Nagarjuni hills, are gadgets of art, architectural structures carved from media. As compositions, they are humanoid structures made to stand on ground, including Forster's tipsy boulder on the mountain-top, Kawa Dol, swaying in the wind, perpetually about to fall off.

Man-made structures (particularly empty
tombs, I find) seldom have within them
the stuff to scare one at all. In Greece
I withstood the *tolos* of Mycenae within
the Cyclopean Walls and the Great Lion
Gate, the wind blowing up a fury beneath
blue sky and black goats roaming about
the gully that claimed part of the palace.

An old man drove with a leather strap
his sheep flock as, flashlights drawn, we
descended into the pitch-black passage
to the cistern (the city's secret resource
in times of siege) and similarly explored
the beehive Tomb of Clytemnestra and
the Treasury of Atreus, virtually scaled-
down versions of the neolithic passage

tomb at Newgrange, Co. Meath, Ireland.
But these chambers are empty, frightless
ruins compared with the *natural,* National
Monuments, or nature-built wonder caves
in our dwindling wilderness. The latter are
due the greatest possible respect. Caverns
measureless with "deep romantic chasms"
are in every way sacred: leave them alone.

On Reading Joyce—Then and Again

(I)

A colleague from Seneca, South Carolina,
touched his forehead to Yeats's tombstone
and felt something strange happen to him.
Later, at home, a portrait of Oscar Wilde,
hanging beside the Sligo bard, tumbled off
its nail to show that Yeats had trans-shifted
across the Pond to perform acrobatics on
a wall nail, peerless in all South Carolina.

Conversely, my first encounter with Ireland
came about on a pilgrimage by trans-Arctic
route from Portland to London (Gatwick),
with an unscheduled refueling in Reykjavik
and, eventually, an overnight boattrain ride
across a choppy Irish Sea to Dún Laoghaire
Harbor and disembarkation past a solitary
lightbulb at an unattended Customs station.

Dublin in 1973 was somehow a throwback
to the fifties—long hemlines, old bicycles,
old cars, trains, autobuses—I liked it though
Ulysses was still censored and unavailable
unless wrapped in bown paper and bought
discreetly at the Book of Kells Exhibition,
the *Tunc* crucifixerant page having featured
in my recent term paper on *Finnegans Wake*.

On *Ulysses*, I got hooked with Telemachus
(a triptych of chapters before Bloom enters)
to the very end of Proteus. Because more
like Buck Mulligan than Stephen, I favored
swimming at the Forty Foot before starting
off a walk from Sandycove to Sandymount
and beyond for at best the first eight miles
of Dedalus *fils'* lyrical Bloomsday odyssey.

A Portrait of the Artist was of course also
about me going off alone as a young man
in quest of a pliable style with which to say
anything worth saying in a modern novel.
It was not enough that the great American
novel had Faulkner, Fitzgerald, Hemingway.
Yet *Ulysses* is about failure, Stephen's not
flying high enough to sustain his epiphanies.

Chamber Music is just a music hall libretto
compared to the delicate *Pomes Penyeach*
and the manuscript lyric *Giacomo Joyce,*
the masterpiece in *vers libre* facsimiled by
Richard Ellmann. In the pyramidal scheme
of *Dubliners,* Joyce built the foundation for
his artist on the astringent stone of Flaubert:
on paralysis as theme, epiphany as method.

So *Ulysses* is also about the artist's capacity
to succeed against paralysis, which I vividly
understood in terms of *poliomyelitis,* defined
literally by my father's inability to rise when
a hot-gospeller laid hands on him in a circus
tent, one summer, in 1953 or '4. In time, this
son believed Joyce to be stellar and art to be
an antidote for faith that surfeits good sense.

(II)

For many years, then, Ireland felt like home
away from home. As Joyce matured enough
to write *Ulysses,* the great day-book fading
into night, he became the mixed metaphor of
Stephen + Bloom ("Blephen" and "Stoom"),
two yolks in the same egg, so that the novel
existed for him in the recreation of imagined
selves impossibly coextant in time and space.

Wherefore, then, should Ithaca suggest to one
a lightbulb in an unattended Customs station?

(a) Because abject objectivity is due to acute
fatigue and to toiling too long into the night.
(b) Because scientific observation, like one's
unsentimental interrogation of the self, as in
a catechism, requires dispassionate phrasing
of questions and answers since the latter are
always already known. (c) Because lightbulbs
alone illuminate little beyond their aloneness.

(d) Because they do not illuminate passers-by
except by their singularity as dead objects. (e)
Because of the complete absence of Authority,
or a body to detect false identities. (f) Because
sea legs had not yet been repurposed for land
navigation on a parfit island, which is to say
Ireland. And, finally, (g) because I was tired,
wanted lodging, a bed, and sheets to the wind.

*Then, as mathematics conduce sleep, how did
numbers come to be used to explain birth as
a slate on which selves divide or paradoxically
combine with factors of* pneuma *and longevity?*

Bloom's alphabetically scrambled rhyming of
imaginary auks' egg collectors shows that—
before his last clause and the Modern Library
Edition's Big Period (•)—counting brings on
sleep by self-hypnotic suggestion. Before that,
Bloom teaches Stephen the relations that exist
between their ages on and from June 16, 1904,
then as ratios, forth and back, through the ages.

On this first Bloomsday, they are 38 and 22,
respectively, a difference of 16 years. But at
Stephen's birth in 1882 (also the year Joyce
was born) the ratio of their ages was 16 to 0,
or 0 by definition; then, incredibly, infinity
from first instant but reduced to 17 by 1883;
to 9 by 1884; to 6.3 by 1885; and to 0.57893
by 1904, although Joyce (as Bloom) worked

out the ratios by inverting the order, making
himself the denominator to juggle the value
of the resulting ratios in spite of the fact that
age difference remains immutably the same.
To make a modest example: although there
are 27 fixed years plus 261 days between my
father and his only son (and nearly that since
he died), those ratios only decline by degree.

So, to take a quantum leap forward, finally,
how do we generally measure Bloom/Elijah
vis-à-vis his throwawy antitype, the Rev. J.
Alexander "Christ" Dowie of the Christian
Catholic Apostolic Church of Zion, Illinois?

Favorably, I should think, as Bloom parodies
in jest without motive to hoodwink his friend.
For example, when art had not been invented
by humans until c. 45,000 BCE, he deadpans
that Blephen and Stoom might have actually
existed, according to calculation, in 81,396
BCE, even though their author would need
to have been born beforehand, an event not

to occur for 83,278 years. On the other hand,
Dowie is wicked, as our eyes plainly see and
ears blanch at the profanity of his type, with
that of the Citizen Cyclops whose good eye
no-man Bloom heroically pokes by taunting
as if by a prophet, the mayor of Flowerville,
New Bloomusalem, a republic rendered quite
honorably in the style of King James's Bible.

At the conclusion of the Oxen of the Sun, the
language of Dowie's leaflets is intoxicating,
one of a huckster's tricks to gull the gullible:
"The Deity ain't no nickel dime bumshow.[...]
You'll need to rise precious early, you sinner
there, if you want to diddle the Almighty God."
And in the Circe episode, Evangelistic Dowie
preaches to The Mob as Joyce seems to have

been aware of the news circulating about how
this huckster (supposed "third manifestation of
Elijah") had taken money from sisters, among
them my father's mother's aunts in Wisconsin
—funds for a temple in Zion City that he never
built, a new "Shiloh Tabernacle" toward which
he planned to do no more than plow a boundary
around a field. Doing genealogy, my daughter

discovered this connection ten years ago while
tracing our Nonconformist family roots from
Somerset and Devon and their migration as a
flock through mid-nineteenth-century Coffee
County, Tennessee, to perch as a kind of sect,
for some years, in Waukesha, Wisconsin. My
great-grandfather, as my Joyce-self for shame
is pleased to report, was their first *breakaway.*

(III)

And does that not, in a way, close the circle?

In 1902, the twenty-year-old James Joyce met
W. B. Yeats (who was only a year older than
Bloom) and said that "I have met you too late.
You are too old," confessing that he himself
lacked only "pure imagination." By that token,
my friend's parable about Oscar Wilde, Yeats,
and the Seneca wall nail absolutely happened
and is true today, except in spirit and politics.

The Triumph of Love

"'But some day I shall be dust too. And—' he spoke now firmly, quietly, with a
kind of triumph: 'who is he who will affirm that there must be a web of flesh
and bone to hold the shape of love?'"
              —William Faulkner, "Beyond" (*Harper's Magazine*, Sept. 1933)

This story's trick is that the narrator,
Judge Howard Allison, Sr., has either
just died and knows it or dreams his
death while a jury deliberates a case
in his court. Either way, after twenty
long years pining for a boy on a pony,
Howard Allison, Jr. ("*April 3, 1903.
August 22, 1913.*"), the judge faces

his interlocutors, the atheist suicide
Mothershed (a student of Voltaire's
Philosophical Dictionary) and "The
Great Agnostic" Robert Ingersoll, also
dead but not hardly a Republican by
marriage like the judge, who stoops in
his pajamas to clear earth away from
the boy's carven name, his *own* name.

The graveyard sequence came alive to
me in the company of my daughter, on
a trip partly dedicated to tracing a single
branch of our family on a grassy bluff
beside the rolling Susquehanna River
(named for the Susquehannock, *people
of the muddy river*) by studying grave
stones of our Fortner/Falconer kinfolk.

My daughter says the surname recalls
distantly some Faulkners who moved
up to Canada in the 1770s as Loyalists,
when our Benjamin Fortner II or III in
Mifflinville, Pennsylvania (born 1758
and buried "in the eightieth year of his
age"), was a Patriot, as attests a medal
driven in the ground next to his grave

and beside my great-grandmother-five-
times-over, his sister, Elizatheth Fortner
Garrison (July 13, 1744; July 13, 1835),
the linchpin of genetic speculation about
Benjamin Fortner I or II and Scotland's
Isabelle Douglas of Bothwell Castle lore,
a lady made poor by pirates, sold in New
Jersey to a planter, and thereafter (as this

planter's son's wife) bore a surfeit of heirs:
Elizabeth Fortner Garrison, Revolutionary
Benjamin II or III, and a passel of siblings,
many moving to the Susquehannock region
to farm for a generation before the next one
drifted to Illinois, California, and Oregon,
where long migration stopped, necessarily,
as good land, a limited resource, ran out.

Even now, there are no easy roads to travel
in Pennsylvania, except along the river, as
we learned *en route* to the 25th International
Conference on Virginia Woolf, Bloomsburg
University, Bloomsburg, PA, having outrun
a tornado on the way up, taking shelter just
in time, and dividing labor between the two
of us: the old professor and the genealogist.

Which brings us to the movement of ghosts
in Faulkner's story and the judge's decision
to forswear both perdition and the promised
reunion with his boy so as not to lose himself:
"because of death, I know that I am," he tells
Ingersoll, as one agnostic to another. "And
that is all the immortality of which intellect is
capable." A procession passes before Judge

Allison like the people Titian painted in the
convention of Petrarch's *Trionfo d'Amore*, an
allegory in which this boy is blindfolded as
winged Cupid, drawn in a chariot pursued by
souls he has enslaved. Bereaved over a death
by runaway pony, the judge decides to join
his boy in the Allison plot, come what may:
"Gentlemen of the Jury, you may proceed."

Silence and Wonder

"He lay still beneath the tarred paper, in a silence filled with fairy patterings. Again his body slanted and slanted downward through opaline corridors groined with ribs of dying sunlight upward dissolving dimly, and came to rest at last in the windless gardens of the sea."
—William Faulkner, "Carcassonne" (1926) from *These 13* (1931)

In "Black Music," we have the first bars of a prelude to a ballet in which the writer has no object other than to entertain, and the fugitive Wilfred Midgleston does that from a hide-out in Rincón, Puerto Rico. Improvisationally, in "Carcassonne," he engages his tired skeleton in free indirect discourse and would gallop to glory on a pony *"with eyes like blue electricity."*

He thinks: *"I want to perform something bold and tragical and austere"*—a thought formed soundlessly from words in "pattering silence," the mind suspended in "lackful contemplation" while his bones slumber serenely "beneath an unrolled strip of tarred roofing made of paper." The first story is Faulkner's "Prélude à l'après-midi d'un '*farn*'" and Midgleston his Nijinsky.

By the same token, the second fable would be (and is) his exquisite "Clair de Lune" poem. At 29 when he wrote it, his voice would not have been right for a draughtsman of Brooklyn nearly six decades absent—for the "clotting of the old gutful compulsions and circumscriptions" of one who had taken to the woods if only for a day as a "farn" or faun. Instead, we have the *person* of

a young man intoxicated by a fresh brush with an old world still alive, after recent war, within the architecture of an ancient citadel with dark corridors and groined arches in southern France, namely the Gallo-Roman Cité de Carcassonne. At that age, more than fifty years later, I knew that Faulkner had given an honest reflection of his own reality and was right to favor that story.

I had picked up the scent of an occult sympathy
from my own experience traveling in Provence
and lodging in Nîmes a few days after finishing
Thomas Bergin's Crofts Classics translation of
The Divine Comedy and excising pages of notes
that I had jotted mechanically on diagrams about
Dante's Hell, Purgatory, and Cosmos, including
a list of "Celestial Orders and Correspondences."

The rest of the book I left in the armoire for the
next pilgrim, who also might be traveling light.
My wife left behind a worn copy of Burckhardt's
Civilization of the Renaissance in Italy because,
shortly, we expected to drill through the massif
by train between Grenoble and Turin. So for days
we had been exploring the *centre ville* of Nîmes,
the Maison Carrée, and the Arènes rededicated to

the sport of bloodless bullfighting. A bus took us
into the Cévennes mountains to amble about on
the aqueduct Pont du Gard for a prospect of cliffs,
spawning trout (49m. below), and aerial views of
tourists braving cold water and tree-bending wind.
Arles came last by way of the Moulin de Daudet,
Saint-Rémy-de-Provence, the "dead city" of Les
Baux carved on a mountain-top, and old Glanum.

To the inland west, Carcassonne arose only after
the founding of Greco-Roman Glanum. Yet time
means nothing to the inscrutable *grottes des fées*
in the Occitanie, where feys may have suggested
a patter of Rincón attic rats—that is, to a genius
mad enough in his bones to imagine a past life as
a Crusader on a phantom horse *"galloping up the
hill and right off into the high heaven of the world."*

The exhausted part of the body ("save that part
which suffered neither insects nor temperature")
might surrender to silence in spite of craving the
"blue precipice never gained." Yet we are told,
in Dante's *Paradise* (Cantos first and last), that
Beatrice gave instructions on "transhumanizing"
without words and on achieving *beatific* status
in human form *squared* to the circle of divinity.

So it was in the Hôtel de Paris, Nîmes, that such
options were imagined in the hour after midnight
in heat without benefit of air-conditioning. Lying
duo on a mattress, we sweated in our skin under
a thin linen sheet and dreamed our own dreams,
content that our one window was secure against
mosquitoes, vile tormentors pursuant to a nasty
misadventure while camping in El Saler, Spain.

(A person learns that *pursuant* and *pursued* differ
although derived from the same radical, meaning
to follow with hostile intent.) In sleep, I assumed
the part of don Alighieri in the plot of a dream of
surpassing beauty until I felt compelled to open
a window, immediately finding that cool air was
already stirring around my body. As if by reflex,
my eyes opened to behold an indistinct figure on

the sill, a crouching shape filling out the window
frame as viewed from my side (or starboard edge)
of the bed. It wore blue jeans under a nightgown
and made speech in a frittering *patois* of French
and English once I stopped directing it to avaunt
and once my wife awoke to recognize its distress,
that of a woman who had crawled along a fourth-
story ledge to enter a dark room, strangely drawn.

This Woman from the Window entered like a cat
but said she'd been chased by an obese man with
russet hair—perhaps the one we found standing
behind the door when we opened it to put her out.
Chaos is the mother of ambiguity. Hence we don't
really know what happened nor how it ended, for
the woman, night clerk, and fat man all vanished
in first light—much as we did too, in point of fact.

Call it serendipity—the wonder is that it happened
at all, like a poem or bad luck. In six weeks' time,
we took a room in the Hotel Ideon Antron almost
straight off the boat in Iraklion—lucky "Rm. 7" in
a Class E pension, where we maintained our daily
average expediture of $27.48 on a side street lined
with tavernas—a street filled with tables by night
and a short walk from the city's Venetian ramparts.

The Cretan sun was merciless, but the island was
free of mosquitoes. Head coverings and a pair of
polarizing sunglasses were the custom as well as
de rigueur for Europeans and Americans bearing
much northern DNA. To wit, Faulkner's tar-paper
invention came to mind on the process of "denning
up" to simplify "the mechanics of sleeping" over
a cantina; a device like "reading glasses which old

ladies used to wear, attached to a cord that rolls
onto a spindle in a neat case" somehow affixed
to "the deep bosom of the mother of sleep." In
extreme heat, a parasol might have proven more
useful in country everywhere in want of shadow.
In the absence of shade cast by a vertical seawall,
for instance, the mind goes wobbly on oscillating
colors observed in the range of raw, white light.

On exploring the ramparts, treading the grounds
and ruins at Knossos, and body-surfing at Malia,
we found that few walls cast shadows deep enough
for two to sit in to snack on peaches, fresh bread,
and the slightly gritty water one drew into a bottle
from the hotel tap. Though we ate well at night, I
thought of the plight of Wilfred Midgleston, *post
restante* Puerto Rico, and wondered: *Am I to die*

*here, then, without so much as a sheet over me on
a bed not more than a worn mattress on a pallet?*
As an omen, the water faucet went dry just as we
expected and as we were departing for Rethymno,
a lovely town of half the size on a sickle-shaped
harbor featuring a small marina, beach cabanas for
bathing, and a Venetian fortezza castle retrofitted
to a mosque by Turks as a bulwark againt pirates.

Our new quarters touted running water and luxury,
including a private shower and toilet, but had no
name apart from the sign "Rent Rooms." In first
excitement, I climbed a minaret joined to a movie-
theater conversion and scouted the grounds of Old
Town as if from a tall tree. Thereafter, closeby our
billet, we swam at the bathing beach, then dined
on chicken, Greek salad, and lemonade beside an

almost slumbering sea—"tumbling peacefully to
the wavering echoes of the tide," the writer said.
We were obviously recharging. So on our second
day I read St. Paul's Epistle to the Hebrews and
purchased copies of Vergil's *Aeneid* and W. H. D.
Rouse's *Gods, Heroes and Men of Ancient Greece*
at a kiosk, where I learned that the IRA had just
assassinated Lord Mountbatten by blowing up his

boat in Sligo, recalling remarks made by a couple
in Co. Galway about bombings that "didn't happen"
in the South anymore, being a problem of the North
that the Irish, not the English, would resolve. While
searching for the owner of a lost dog, we discovered
a restaurant with an abridged title ("Samaria Rest.")
and embraced the notion that we were Samaritans—
a premise that even hardship acquitted wonderfully.

What Price Paradise

In Cuernavaca, Acapulco, and Mexico City, from late 1936 to July 1938, Malcolm Lowry wrote the first draft of his one masterpiece, *Under the Volcano*—and in succeeding drafts 2, 3, 4 (executed in isolation during the war) foreclosed on the idea that Paradise, or sheer happiness, can be secured at a price without one's characters flipping off of the carnival

wheel, mistaking immolation for abnegation. But for himself, as he finished the work with a second wife, Margerie, he hoped the novel might be mistaken, and eventually advanced that claim with a piece of lyrical auto fiction called "The Forest Path to the Spring," albeit posthumously published and about happiness attained in the execution of his compositions.

Most of those would never be anything more than second-rate next to the "symphony" that he had written, with Margerie (to her credit), "but at least as it seemed [...] there was room for them in the world": an irony to appreciate in the cramped world she and Lowry inhabited within a series of shacks, one of which burned to total loss save for 40 poems and the novel.

After the fire, he tried to invoke in his writing the notion that "the experience of one happy man might be useful" to somebody, observing "rain like a bead curtain falling behind a gap in the trees," each drop like a life, or "medium of life," "producing a circle in the ocean," each "widening to infinity." British Columbia and hard living on an inlet stretched taut his canvas.

The landscape, flora, and weather in Dollarton
(aka "Eridanus," Lowry's utopian village) are
a very kindred habitat for my people—viewed
from a distance of 300 miles, 5 hours by car, or
only 4 degrees tallied by latitude. The opposite
may be said of Cuernavaca, spot-on the 19th
parallel, host of twin volcanoes, 18 churches,
57 cantinas, and 400 grand swimming pools.

In *Under the Volcano*, the players must all be
counterpointed and sacrificed. As the Consul
and his brother are both Lowry *alter egos*, so
Yvonne, the Consul's wife, is the projection
of both Lowry's wives, past and present, for
the construction of a love-triangle, or, rather,
a diagonally bisected square, with Lowry at
opposing points, the wives drawn at tangent.

In execution, one concedes that a writer may
sometimes overbuild a novel with too much
tension when casualties may not be necessary
to supply all the ingredients of a tragedy. To
toss a dead dog after the Consul into the hell
gate of the *barranca*, then to stampede horses
through it to signify death and apotheosis in
marriage—images of birds migrating toward

constellations studied from the porch of a lost
house, star-points eddying in rings on water—
such art, in fine, demands a serious answer to
the question, *Is it possible to rent but not own
Paradise for $12 a month?* They could afford
no more, and *found* Paradise didn't seem right
to keep when people were dying in war. Being
abject in the eyes of the world, there could be

no "nonsense about love in a cottage," about
being "happy within oneself" when the "world
outside—so portentous in its prescriptions for
[a] man of imaginary needs that were in reality
his damnation—was hell." While toting water
from the spring to the shack exacted a toll, the
bearer grew stronger by it. Like rent, the act
purchased life and satisfaction for a duration,

even (in the writer's journal-like account of it)
the grit to stand-off a mountain lion with a few
chosen words: "Brother, it's true. I like you in
a way, but just the same, between you and me,
get going!" On the first carry, a full moon had
risen "like a burning thistle" over the cougar's
mountains. In the end, the forest path gained in
significance as the way to the brook, Lowry's

spring (the same word for the wilding season)
bubbling up from an underground source. This
path leads to the "golden kingdom" of beasts,
as reading tells us, but also to such other paths
by which "one loses one's way, paths that not
merely divide but become the twenty-one paths
that lead back to Eden." "Laughing," he says to
us, "we stooped down to the spring and drank."

Applesauce, or the Origin of Irony

For a few years (because that is all there were
ever going to be), summers were long, winters
short between the quarantining of my father at
hospital and sale of the family homestead *out
of family*—a five years' arc of childhood that
I try to put together from memories past recall.

These memories commence from the day Dad
affixed a hand-brake to the Chevy sedan and
taught himself to drive all over again. A drive
to the "home place" for his parents to observe
his newfound mobility was a triumph for him
and invitation for the tribe to muster as a body.

They did, although I remember a fierce brow
in the rearview mirror and stern words against
his father for spitting tobacco juice from the
backseat window as the poles of male authority
reversed, allowing that even a father might be
reprimanded by a son for childish indecorum.

One standard regulation for the grandchildren
was that we were not to "go down to the *crick*,"
by which was meant a tiny creek that bordered
the derelict stumpfield of a neighbor's property.
Naturally, we strayed down to this wild thread
of briars and sleeping night creatures anyway.

Often in twos or threes for courage and to bear
witness if somebody told, we ventured down-
hill to a draw where green saplings clustered
around both sides of a trickle-falls that dropped
perhaps three feet from a shallow outcropping
of stone into an oval pool the color of red clay.

I can't recall ever touching that water unless it
was with a stick, which was evidently the best
way not to get into trouble when there were so
many other ways to do that. And maybe it was
a good thing that I seldom got caught and had
to pretend, bent over a wheelchair, that it hurt.

My grandfather was not one to discipline his
children, for, as Dad said, if one of them had
broken a leg by falling from a tree, there was
no one to blame, and injury was punishment
enough. I was told that an infraction could be
allayed by suspending a boy in a gunnysack.

And this was from a winch in the hayloft, so
the child learned never to do the deed again,
which must have been serious, a kept secret.
My dad once fell asleep in a horse's manger
while evading punishment and was awarded
the nickname "Pete," the dray horse's name.

Swept clean and in disuse, the hayloft—aerie
of rafter pidgeons and barn owls—naturally
became another forbidden place we loved to
explore, avoiding aged splinterwood and bird
eggs as we dared its dizzying heights. Below,
cracked harness still held the scent of horses.

We were also not permitted to climb about on
rusty implements parked in the weeds and in
the yard around the empty pig shed—an "Old
West" wagon with spokes and broken tongue;
a harrow from Jesus's era with a catapult seat
from which we steered those phantom horses.

We did many things while the adults *talked* in
the house—kid games played loudly and long
into night in shadows cast eerily by yard lights.
Of course, danger is only a matter of scale for
little people whose care is usually a mother's,
an aunt's, or (rarely for me) *this* grandmother's.

She was an enigma that everyone loved, plain
but not simple, sweet but with an arm that had
famously thrown a knife in the direction of one
of her two surviving daughters to stop a fight—
so strongly thrown that it stuck in the linoleum
floor before them. She'd had seven to discipline.

One came and passed, in two weeks less than
a year, "Just [...] to show how | Sweet a flower
in Paradise | would bloom," as said his epitaph
beneath a stone lambkin in the cemetery half-
way up Parrot Mountain. A bad son and gifted
daughter followed that track as young adults.

I only knew their mother as the grandson who
shared the coincidence of our having had the
measles and being kept from school on our 6th
birthdays, respectively, in 1890 and 1956. And
when she called from the side-porch, it was to
be summoned for slices of warm banana bread.

There were no bananas in her garden, but some
of her grandchildren were granted the privilege
of weeding it under her supervision. (Just so, I
planted fruit trees and gardened at home, at my
dad's direction, and understood exactly where
that came from.) The "place" was in her name.

Although her tools were worn, her finest work
was suited to a knife sharpened so many times
that her wrist and mind had grown accustomed
to its curves. At the time, I may not have been
much taller than the barley, but I was called to
sit beside her on a restrung hide-bottom chair,

and there, with the vista of the valley and hills
before us, was taught the art of properly paring,
coring, and slicing apples for pie without cuts
or injury. It was an "adult" skill, and, at 7 or 8,
I was deemed old enough to do it right—or to
make applesauce if the apples were not up to it.

Chapmans do not use insecticide, so the apples
have worms. Thence most peeling and coring
leads to applesauce, requiring strong wrists and
dexterity to separate the good from the bad, also
an observant brain to carve off the mealy parts
and bruises—all right sport for an eventual poet.

As most metaphors end up in the pail for peels,
just so this woman was a mentor in a way she
probably never imagined, either then or when
the census of faces was taken by an in-law, my
mother, in the anniversary photographs of 1957—
4 offspring yet alive, 16 grandkids ages mixed.

My dad honored his folks by making a golden,
spray-painted tree with 50 silver dollars within
bell-shaped envelopes for a centerpiece beside
a white cake his mother didn't bake. Neighbors
came to the big house some had helped to build
but had left unfinished where the children slept.

The next year was about our best year as kids,
for the year after was a catastrophe of strokes,
heart attacks, deaths, a broken hip from a fall
on crutches—a year of grim shocks. But 1958
was the long summer of applesauce, sleeping
in a feather bed, and bicycle stunts for cousins.

In the fall, I was allowed to climb the A-frame
fruit-picking ladder to pick for the cider press,
crab apples for pectin and such. The trees were
ancient and brittle. In turns at the ciderwheel, I
proved strong for a boy; and I learned by almost
drowning at the river the wisdom of swimming.

In December, a walker was made out of linked
water pipe and caster wheels from an old baby
buggy. And in February, Gran lost the cowboy
whose picture she carried in her locket, and lost
another daughter. By mid-summer, she seemed
lost within herself, on a camp stool in her black

Sunday dress, gazing over the river beyond the
pool and picnic grounds at the hot springs, as a
western monarch butterfly (*Danaus plexippus*)
mistook her hat for a clump of milkweed flowers
and perched there for a long time, like a canary
or a pet a grandmother might keep in her house.

By winter, she was gone permanently, and then
the place had to be *liquidated* as there were too
many shares of the estate to divide up between
the heirs of siblings already dead. At first, land
and everything on it was rented out. But the barn
fell in a windstorm, and the house burned down.

So, ironically, 60-some acres were sold as "view
property" to a rich man who dreamed of running
an equestrian stable for *his kind* and a stud-farm
for the conception of thoroughbreds. His idea of
farming meant miles of white-board fencing. To
be sure, there has to be a place in heaven where,

as W. Blake said, "Contrarieties are equally True."

Seeds for Spring

Soon butterflies will go
extinct in this old world.
After a cancer diagnosis,
you might imagine one to
be just a bug with wings
were you to see it flit by.

Imagine, if you will, the
world of poetry without
the *work-lust* of Heaney
and Gary Snyder's "Hay
for Horses," even Yeats's
"Sailing to Byzantium."

You can't, which is why
(though many bugs have
wings) only a few become
royalty—why a cabbage
white rarely feasts beside
those milkweed monarchs.

By the same token, maybe
all plants are meant to be
eaten by certain creatures.
But if there is no god, only
plants, why must they be
eaten to free their *karma*?

Makes no sense—free for
what?—to do over life in
the belly of another form,
another person as in *metem-
psychosis* and to err with
the same stupid mistakes,

ad infinitum, re-glimpsing,
perhaps, the past through
a channel in the Wayback
Machine, never moving on.
Yet if there's a *logic* to it,
it's gone to hell in politics

(as the swing states have
now decreed). So, indeed,
what is to become of us?
I'm with Voltaire and the
poets and choose to act by
plotting out another work.

I will make another garden
book, a cultivation without
theory but with intention
to endure uncertainty that
looms in winter—the work
of saving seeds for spring.

A Note on the Author

Wayne K. Chapman is Professor Emeritus of English at Clemson University, and is now living with his family in Portland, Oregon—a native son of four generations. He is the author/editor of 17 books and numerous articles on W. B. Yeats, Leonard and Virginia Woolf, Irish scholar-poets Edward Dowden and Elizabeth Dickinson West, and William Wordsworth and Samuel Taylor Coleridge. Chapman taught at Clemson for twenty-five years, edited *The South Carolina Review* for twenty, and directed Clemson University Press for sixteen as its executive editor. He has also read poetry and fiction for *The Timberline Review*, as one of its rotating associate editors-in-chief (2018). This is his first collection of poetry, and he prays it won't be his last.

♣

www.ingramcontent.com/pod-product-compliance
Lightning Source LLC
Chambersburg PA
CBHW061416090426
42742CB00026B/3481